Contents

KW-481-073

1 Rats and Mice in their Millions 7

2 Where Rats Came From 17

3 The Brown Rat 21

4 The Black Rat 27

5 Rats Worldwide 31

6 The House Mouse is Everywhere 39

7 More British Mice 47

8 Some American Mice 57

9 Mice in the Tropics 61

10 The Sleepy Dormouse 65

11 The Mysterious Mole-rat 72

Glossary 75

Finding Out More 78

Picture Credits 79

Index 80

Rats and Mice

Harvest mice climb through
a forest of wheat stalks.

Rats and Mice

Ralph Whitlock

Priory Press Limited

Young Naturalist Books

Squirrels
Foxes
Bats
Rabbits and Hares
Hedgehogs
Frogs and Toads
Snakes and Lizards
Badgers
Deer
Spiders
Otters
Rats and Mice
Stoats and Weasels
Birds of Prey

SBN 85078 185 X
Copyright © 1974 Priory Press Ltd
First published in 1974 by
Priory Press Ltd
101 Grays Inn Rd, London WC1
Filmset by Keyspools Ltd, Golborne, Lancs.
Printed in Great Britain by
The Pitman Press, Bath.

1 : Rats and Mice in their Millions

Rats and mice are animals which we are bound to have seen wherever we live. They are as common in towns as in the country. Maybe you have kept white rats and mice as pets; they are different only in shade and tameness from their wild cousins. Pet mice and rats are bright, active and quite intelligent animals, and wild rats and mice are like them. However, people think of them as dirty, and they are usually detested because of the damage they do.

Rats and mice are *rodents*, or gnawing animals. Their two pairs of long front teeth, known as *incisors*, are strong and well coated with enamel, enabling them to gnaw through some of the hardest substances. Rats have been known to eat through concrete, lead pipes, sheet aluminium, earthenware drainpipes and the metal sheaths of cables.

Rats and mice have discovered that food is to be found wherever men go, and so they follow men everywhere. European rats have spread to the tropics, where they have multiplied very rapidly in the hot climate. At one time they became so numerous that they almost ruined

Opposite : A garden dormouse pokes its head out of a hollow tree trunk.

This shows what damage rats can do. Here they have gnawed their way through a lead pipe.

the sugar industry in the West Indies. They have likewise followed men to the Arctic, where they have grown thick coats of fur to enable them to stand the long winters. By climbing aboard ships, often by mooring ropes or cables, they have travelled to distant islands where they have, in some places, almost wiped out many of the local birds and animals.

The mouse's sharp teeth can chew their way through all kinds of things in a very short time.

A Brown rat eats grain stored in a barn.

There are millions upon millions of rats and mice in the world. One estimate puts the number of Brown rats (which are the commonest ones) in temperate countries as being about equal to the human population. That would mean between fifty and sixty million Brown rats in Great Britain, and 200 million in the United States.

The harsh realities of a mouse's life and death. A mouse sniffs at a mousetrap which has already snapped shut and killed another.

But no-one really knows. In tropical countries rats are even more numerous.

When we think of rats and mice we think chiefly of the common Brown rat and the House mouse. As well as these, however, there are over a thousand other kinds of rats and mice, and many of them are very common too.

A saucerful of baby Brown rats, two or three days old.

One of the chief reasons why rats are so plentiful is that they breed so fast. A female Brown rat produces five or six litters a year, and even more if she can find cosy winter quarters. Each litter consists of from five to fifteen young rats, sometimes even more. An average of sixty youngsters each year for each adult female would be a fair estimate.

Rats become mature enough to breed when two months old, so if the first litter is born in March the youngsters from it are ready to start breeding in May. The *gestation* period, or time between mating and the birth of the young, is sixteen to twenty-one days.

If we assume that half the young rats in each litter are female, we can calculate that each of the five females in that first litter will produce four litters of her own before the end of the year. That, at an average of ten per litter, would be forty more rats. The females of her first two litters at least would themselves be breeding before Christmas. Then there would be other females from the later litters of the first female. You may like to work out just how many rats will be running about in December from that pair which started breeding in March. The answer will be over 3,000.

Similar calculations could be made for other kinds of rats and mice. House mice start to breed at the age of six weeks and so can increase in numbers even faster than rats.

Why is the world not completely overrun by rats and mice, so as to leave no room for any other animals, including humans? The reason is the very high mortality rate, which is said to be often as high as 95%. In other words, of all those rats and mice born during the course of a year, 95 out of every 100 die. And, of course, most of them die when very young, before they can start breeding, so the number of young from one pair during a year is never as high as it could be.

Rats and mice have a role in nature which must seem unfortunate and unfair to them. They are the chief food of an enormous number of *carnivorous*, or flesh-eating, creatures. Hawks, owls, foxes, stoats, cats, dogs, crows and many other creatures all feed largely on rats and mice. And men try their best to destroy rats and mice, because of the damage they do.

Rats and mice will eat almost anything. They love any food that humans eat and therefore try to get into any places where food is stored. They will also eat garden crops, berries, nuts, almost every kind of growing plant, and anything made from plants such as ropes, clothes and hay. They will gnaw such unlikely things as soap, candles and various articles made of wood. Rats will kill and eat any defenceless animals or birds, such as young ones in a nest. They will even eat their own young.

One of the worst enemies of rats and mice, and a great friend of mankind: a barn owl flies off with a Long-tailed Field mouse.

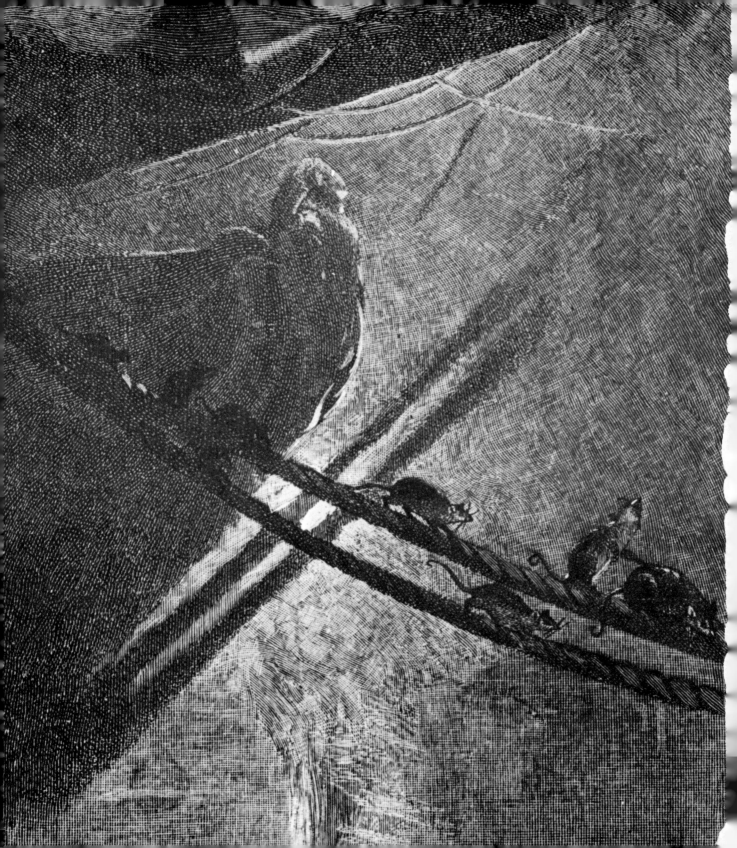

2 : Where Rats Came From

If we had lived in Britain or America a thousand years ago we would never have seen a Brown or Black rat. Both of the two kinds of rats which have now spread over the world came originally from Central Asia. The Black rat was the first to arrive. It is thought that it came to western Europe in the 12th century – that is, between 1100 and 1200 A.D. The Brown rat turned up six hundred years later, in the century after 1700 A.D. A naturalist, Thomas Pennant, wrote in 1776, "This animal never made its appearance in England till about forty years ago."

Another 18th century naturalist, Peter Pallas, spent six years, from 1768 to 1774, exploring Central Asia, from the river Volga as far east as Mongolia. He told a story of how, in 1727, an earthquake in central Asia started immense armies of Brown rats migrating westwards. In huge numbers they swam the Volga and began to move across Russia. Two years later the first ones began to reach England. Their spread was, of course, made quicker by their habit of stowing away on ships whenever possible.

Opposite : Rats leave a ship by running along the ropes and hawsers.

Less is known about the spread of the Black rat, because its chief migrations took place at an earlier period when fewer records were kept. It is known to have come from the same region, Central Asia, and to have become a serious pest in Europe in the 13th and 14th centuries. It is generally thought to have come to western Europe with returning Crusaders, probably in their baggage. The rats which made themselves such a nuisance in the town of Hamelin till beguiled away by the Pied Piper, in Robert Browning's poem, were Black rats.

Rats continue their journeys across the world. They travelled west across America with the waggons of early settlers. They are still moving northwards over the Canadian prairies. The whaling stations on the edge of Antarctica have them. Troopships took them to numerous Pacific islands during the Second World War.

It is when they find a congenial home on an island that rats can be most dangerous. There is a dreadful story about North Rona, a lonely islet in the Atlantic about midway between the Hebrides and the Shetlands. In 1685 about thirty people lived there, dwelling in stone houses built against earth banks so that they were partly underground. A year or two later rats swam ashore from a shipwreck. Finding shelter in burrows around the houses, they ate all the barley meal and other food stored by the people. Eventually everybody starved to death, the last woman being afterwards found, with her baby in her

Black rats high in the roof of a barn. Brown rats prefer to live at ground level, Black rats in roofs.

arms, both lying dead on the rocky shore. Then the rats died of starvation too.

Even more feared than the damage done by the rats themselves are the diseases they carry. The Black Death, or bubonic plague, which carried off at least a third of the entire population of western Europe in the late 1340s was

19

This loaf of bread has been visited by a family of mice!

carried by the Black rat, or rather, by the rat fleas which infest the Black rat. This disease is still common in southern Asia, parts of Africa and South America.

Several other diseases are carried by rats and mice. They are more widespread in the tropics than in temperate climates, but everywhere rats and mice can foul foodstuffs with their droppings and so spread unpleasant illnesses and parasites.

3: The Brown Rat

The Brown rat, like most other rats and mice, has a body designed for pushing through narrow holes. It has a pointed nose, wedge-shaped head and sleek, streamlined body. Its legs are short, and its tail long and tapering. When looking for food the Brown rat creeps along with its stomach nearly touching the ground and its nose stuck out. Its long whiskers are continually twitching, and its beady eyes are placed so that it can see in nearly every direction.

In the countryside the Brown rat lives in burrows, sometimes dug by itself and sometimes taken over from other animals. From its burrow it travels to various feeding places by well marked tracks or runs. It likes to keep under cover if possible, rather than cross open spaces. When it finds food in the open it will, when convinced that it is safe, dart forward, seize a mouthful and retreat quickly to cover. It is quick to spot anything new in familiar surroundings and is very suspicious. That is one reason why it is very hard to trap rats.

The body of the Brown rat is eight or nine inches long.

A Brown rat slinks cautiously from its hole in the ground.

The tail, which is scaly, is about the same length. Its fur is greyish brown, but the ears, feet and tail are hairless and flesh coloured. The underparts are greyish.

As we have already mentioned (see page 13), rats are mature enough to breed at the age of two months. Female rats produce six litters a year during the summer in a temperate climate, more in a hot climate or in places where they can find warm winter quarters. The number of young in each litter is usually between five and fifteen, though one of twenty-three has been recorded.

The young rats are born blind and naked, in a nest roughly made of any available material by the mother.

Rats usually hide by day and come out only at night. If they are cornered they will bite.

A Brown rat gnaws away at a stick. They eat almost anything.

They open their eyes when between two and three weeks old. The nest is usually well hidden, partly from fear of the male rat, which is at times a cannibal and may eat his own young.

In towns Brown rats will live in any place which offers them food and shelter. Although they will skilfully run across ropes and cables to get to any place where they want to go, they are not great climbers. In buildings they tend to live at ground level or under the ground rather than in the roof. They love water, however, and can swim well. Indeed, they are never found too far from water, for, unlike some small animals, they need to drink frequently. In cities many rats live all their lives in sewers.

In the countryside rats generally move into the woods

This Brown rat is grooming itself thoroughly. But although they may clean themselves, they carry disease to people all over the world.

A Black rat hurries up a rope, gripping it with its long-fingered claws.

and fields during the summer. In autumn, when the food supply is becoming exhausted, they move back to farm buildings or even to the nearest town.

Sometimes, when the summer weather has been very good, there is a population explosion of rats. There seem to be rats everywhere. At such times one may see large rat migrations. Scores or hundreds of rats trek across country, looking for new food supplies. To meet a small army of rats on the move is terrifying.

Rat population explosions are usually accompanied by a rapid increase in numbers of the creatures which prey on rats. Owls, stoats, weasels, hawks and foxes become more numerous than usual. So the rat population is forced back to normal again.

Men try to keep the rat population under control by gassing, trapping and poison, as well as by keeping domestic animals such as cats, dogs and mongooses, which kill rats. In spite of all such efforts, the number of rats continues to rise.

4: The Black Rat

The Black rat is slightly smaller and more slender than the Brown rat. It is seven or eight inches long, with a tail about the same length. Its muzzle is more pointed, its ears and eyes larger. As its name implies, the Black rat has black fur – a glossy black, though with a sprinkling of

Black rats live under floorboards, behind partitions and beams and in wall spaces.

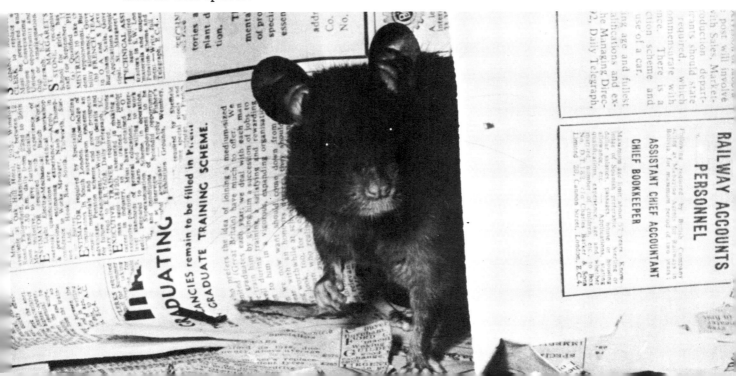

grey hairs. The underparts are dark grey. Tail, ears and paws are hairless. Its tail is scaly, like the Brown rat's, and its paws are pink.

The breeding habits of the Black rat are much the same as those of the Brown rat. The gestation period tends to be slightly longer, and the young take a little longer to reach maturity.

When the Black rat arrived in western Europe, probably in the 12th century, it quickly spread to towns, villages and isolated farms. The Black Death, of which it carried the germs, thus struck everywhere. Black rats prefer towns, however, and now in Britain they are only found there.

Although there seems to be no reason to suppose that Brown rats make a point of fighting Black rats, if such a battle took place the larger, heavier and perhaps more aggressive Brown rat would almost certainly win. When there is competition for a limited amount of food, the Brown rat usually gets whatever food is going. So the Black rat has disappeared from many places where it was once common, including the English countryside.

It survives in towns, especially in large ports, because there the two kinds of rats seem to have a natural division of territory. The Brown rat, as we have seen, lives at ground level and under the ground. The Black rat, which is a good climber, lives in the roofs. *Roof rat* is another name for it. Yet another name is the *Ship rat*, because it

Opposite: This picture clearly shows the claws which make the Black rat so agile.

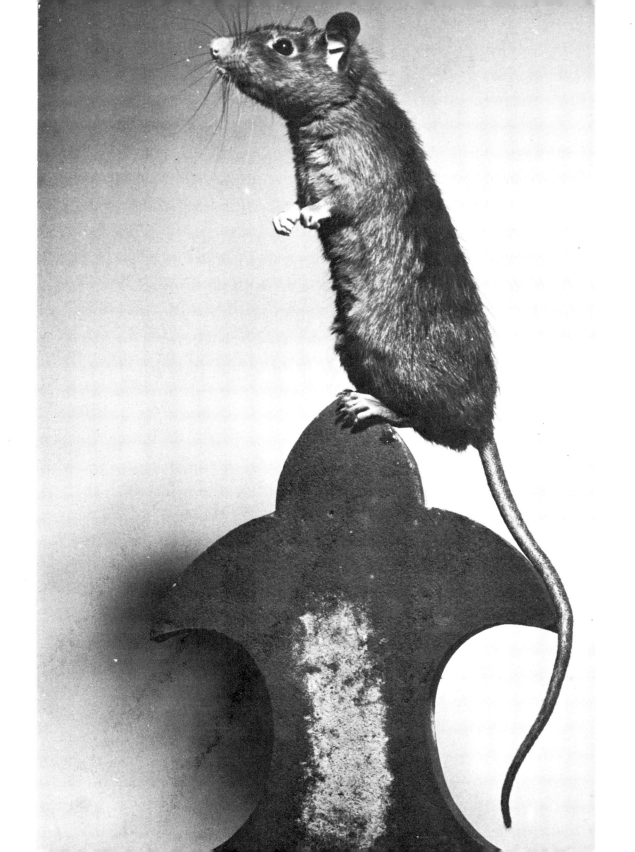

haunts ships and dock warehouses. In the winter of 1941–42 a campaign was launched against the rats which were doing much damage to food in the Port of London, and 81% of the rats caught were Black rats.

Although Black rats, like Brown rats, are found in most countries of the world, they are more at home in hot countries. In India many of them live in trees. In their fur live the fleas which carry the bubonic plague, which is still quite common in many Eastern lands.

Two unusual forms of the Black rat are sometimes found in western Europe. One has cream-coloured or whitish underparts and sometimes white paws and is known as the *Tree rat*. The other is the *Alexandrine rat*, which has a brown back and dusky underparts. The tame White rat, bought in pet shops, is thought to be an albino variety of the Black rat, not of the Brown rat.

5 : Rats Worldwide

Though no other kinds of rat are so widespread as the Brown and Black rats, many others are equally numerous in their own countries. In tropical forests rats are abundant. Many of them live in streams and swamps; others in trees.

A Swamp rat by his nest in the trunk of a dead tree. *Left:* A female white rat and her young.

The Cane rat, also called the Grass Cutter, lives in Africa and is as big as a large rabbit.

Among the tree-dwelling rats are the *Mosaic-tailed rats*, of which there are several kinds. The scales on their tails are arranged in a mosaic pattern which enables the rats to grip the smaller branches, just as some monkeys do. Such tails are called *prehensile*.

Many of the water-loving or *aquatic* rats have webbed feet. Their shape is flattened a bit, to fit them for life in the water, and their fur is dense and soft, like a seal's. Most forest rats feed at night. The rats of swamp and stream feed on shellfish, frogs, small fish and small birds, as well as the things which other rats normally eat.

The European water vole, by the way, which is often called the water rat, is not a rat at all but a vole, and so is not dealt with in this book.

One of the largest of all rats is the *Giant rat*, which lives in forests in East Africa. It is twenty-seven inches long, with a tail fourteen inches long. Its colour is much the same as that of the Brown rat, but it has white under-parts, white paws and a white tip to its tail. Other giant rats, of much the same size, are found in New Guinea.

The *Cane rat* is another large species. Its length is from fifteen to twenty inches, but its tail is short, usually about three or four inches. It is an ugly, heavily built animal with bristly hair. Its incisors, or gnawing teeth, are bright orange. It lives mostly on the edge of lakes and rivers, eating water plants, but often it invades plantations of sugar cane and does much damage. Its home is in Africa. Local people consider it very good to eat.

A large rat found in and around houses in tropical Africa is the *Giant Pouched rat*. It is sixteen inches long and has a seventeen-inch tail. It derives its name from its cheek pouches, in which it can store food when it finds a supply which needs to be eaten quickly. A curious thing about this rat is that, whereas the fur of most rats is infested with fleas, mites and other small creatures, it has a parasitic cockroach, found apparently on no other animal.

America has many rats of its own. Among the commonest are the *Pack rats*, of which there are several kinds. They are of much the same size and colour as the Brown rat but have different habits. One habit is to build large

33

Above : A Desert rat coming up out of its hole. *Left :* The Giant Pouched rat stores food in pouches in its cheek.

houses of sticks, often with several rooms in them. Another is to collect brightly-coloured objects for ornamenting its nests. Pack rats in the southern states of the U.S.A. live in and among cactus plants, eating the juicy fruit and stems. They protect their burrows with fortifications of stones and prickly cactus!

The *Cotton rat* is like the Black rat rather than the Brown rat in colour and size. It is found in the southern states of U.S.A. and throughout Central America and the northern countries of South America. It breeds even more rapidly than the European rats, and as a result its population reaches a peak about once in five years. The rats are then attacked by a disease, and their population declines. Cotton rats are mature enough to start breeding

35

The curious Kangaroo rat of North America, which never drinks, and leaps like a kangaroo.

at the age of one month. They breed all the year round and often have as many as eight or ten young in a litter. Usually there is only about a month between the production of each litter.

America has many species of *Rice rat*, which live chiefly by the water in coastal districts. They are smaller than the

Cotton rat, but often become serious pests. They are especially fond of eating rice.

One type of country not much liked by rats is desert land. This is because most rats need plenty of water. However, some kinds have adapted themselves to life in the desert.

One is the *Sand rat*, of North Africa. It lives in *wadis*, or dry river beds, and eats cacti and other succulent plants.

The *Kangaroo rats* of North America never drink. Their bodies are adapted to get enough moisture from the dry plants which they eat. Because they have no sweat glands they do not lose water by evaporation. In the heat of the day they retire to sleep in burrows, away from the fierce sun. Their name comes from their long legs, on which they leap like kangaroos.

In the desert-like Nullarbor Plain of Australia the *Stick-nest rat* lives in colonies. These rats look like rabbits, because they have long ears and blunt noses, but they have rat-like tails. They built huge nests of sticks, often around a stunted bush, and dozens of rats live together in them.

In the Nile valley the *Nile Grass rat* lives in the open fields, eating grass and rice during the growing season. When the annual drought begins, it retires into the great cracks which appear in the rock-hard ground. There it is safe not only from carnivorous animals but from the fires with which the farmers burn the dead grass.

37

A House mouse on the alert, before coming out into the open.

6: The House Mouse is Everywhere

It is strange to think of the common and abundant House mouse as a foreigner, but it is. Its original home seems to have been the plains of Central Asia. Everywhere else it has been introduced by man. Not deliberately, of course. It has travelled in baggage, ships, waggons and food stores. It has been said that a mouse can live its whole life in a single bag of flour.

The travels of the House mouse began, however, much earlier than those of the Black and Brown rats. It spread across Europe in prehistoric times. From there it has travelled to every part of the world. It has even settled in Antarctica, where it shares the huts of the scientists who live there.

For an animal which can live and breed in a cold store, the climate of Antarctica is not too harsh. House mice have been found flourishing in cold stores, in which the temperature never rises above 17°F. (minus 10°C.), in London and other places. They live there in almost total darkness. They eat the frozen meat stored there and make their nests, often in the meat carcasses themselves, out of the hessian in which the meat is wrapped. Yet they seem remarkably fit. They grow thick, glossy fur and become fatter and heavier. Strangely, too, the females have more litters a year and, on average, more babies in each litter.

The House mouse has become essentially a hanger-on of human communities. Although it can adapt itself to extreme conditions in man-made surroundings, such as those in a cold store, it is not so good at living in places without man. The tiny island of St. Kilda, 70 miles or so out in the Atlantic off the west coast of Scotland, had its own special population of House mice. They had lived there so long, sharing the houses of the people and feeding in the grain stores, that they had become different in several small ways from the House mice that live on the mainland. But when the people of St. Kilda were evacuated from their lonely island in 1930, leaving it uninhabited, the St. Kilda mice soon died out.

Other islands, however, have races of House mice which seem to have adapted themselves to living on their own. The island of Skokholm, off the coast of Pembrokeshire, has a flourishing population of mice living in burrows in its cliffs.

House mice which came along with soldiers during the Second World War to the Galapagos Islands, off the coast of Ecuador, played havoc with the local population of birds, insects and plants. They ate so much that some of the local birds and animals starved to death.

Opposite : Creeping into the kitchen.

Above: A mouse grooms itself. *Left:* Even when eating they are constantly on the alert.

Compared to the Brown and Black rats, the House mouse is a dainty and gentle little animal. We must not be too sentimental about it, however, for, like the rats, it carries diseases and contaminates food with its droppings, as well as eating much food which we need for ourselves.

The length of the House mouse is three or four inches, with a tail about as long again. It has large ears, large,

A handful of baby House mice. Normally five or six are born at a time.

bright eyes, and a pointed muzzle that is well equipped with whiskers and is always twitching. Its senses of hearing, sight and smell are acute. Its fur is brownish grey, with the underparts rather lighter. Its tail is almost bare.

In buildings House mice can find many holes and cracks in which to hide and sleep and make their nests. The young are born in a nest of soft, dry vegetable matter, such as hay, straw or fabrics like sacking and clothes, shredded up by the mother mouse.

The *gestation* period, or time between mating and the

birth of the young, is two to three weeks. The young are born naked and blind. They are weaned at three weeks. The average number of litters per year is said to be five or six under "natural" conditions, which means for mice living in the countryside, but it varies considerably for town mice. If a House mouse can find a warm store or other building, where the temperature does not vary all the year round, it will keep on breeding without a break for winter. The litters it will produce under such conditions will also be larger. Under "natural" conditions in the countryside the breeding season is from March to October. The litters tend to be smaller at the beginning and end of the season, when they average five or six young, rising to over ten per litter in summer. Young mice can start breeding at six weeks.

In the countryside House mice often leave houses and buildings and go out into the fields and woods for the summer, feeding on plants, seeds and berries. Autumn sees them moving back to the farms and villages again. When nearly all harvested corn was stored in sheaves in ricks, the mice found the ricks a perfect home for the winter. There, in cosy nests in the straw, they kept breeding right through the winter, until the ricks seemed to be alive with mice. Sometimes they ate as much as half the grain in the rick. Now that the grain is threshed in the field by combine harvesters, the mice have to try to find their way into the granaries where it is stored.

45

The trap has been set off, and there is not much time to escape!

When mice are settled in a place, they choose their own special feeding territories, marking the boundaries with urine, as a dog does. It is these boundary marks which we can smell when our nose tells us that a place is infested with mice.

Cats, stoats, weasels and other carnivorous animals can also smell the mice and hurry to the feast. Weasels are small enough to enter mouse burrows and kill them there. The mortality rate among mice is probably at least as high as for Brown rats, and the adult House mouse has a shorter life than the rat. Few live longer than eighteen months, and most die in their first winter.

7 : More British Mice

The other fairly common British mouse is the Long-tailed Field mouse, or Wood mouse. It is a little larger than the House mouse and is much brighter to look at. Its sleek fur is reddish brown or golden fawn, with white underparts.

The Long-tailed Field mouse is the mouse of the countryside, just as the House mouse is the mouse of the town. It lives all the year round in woods and fields. It feeds mainly by night, spending the day in the burrows it tunnels for itself just under the surface of the soil.

Its food consists of acorns, berries, roots, grain, fruit, vegetables and almost every edible sort of plant. In autumn it makes stores of nuts and other food for use in the winter. These stores are often in a side burrow, next to the living quarters of the mouse colony. Long-tailed Field mice are *gregarious*, which means that they live in groups. The stores are made by a number of mice and shared by the whole group in winter.

The nest, which is made of dried grass and other dry vegetable matter shredded by the mice, is not kept just as a nursery but is often occupied by the whole group. It is

47

Above : The Long-tailed Field mouse or Wood mouse. *Left :* Leaning down to feed on a ripe blackberry. The mouse eats only the inner seed and leaves the outerpart.

quite large, often measuring as much as six inches across.

Living as it does in the countryside, the Long-tailed Field mouse has its breeding programme regulated by the seasons. The first litters are born in spring, the last ones in late autumn. Often as many as six litters a year are produced. The number of young per litter rises from four or five in the first ones to six or seven at the peak of the summer season. The gestation period is 25 or 26 days, and mating occurs within a few hours of the birth of a litter. The young are mature enough to breed when a few months old. Few Long-tailed Field mice live longer than one year.

A Long-tailed Field mouse eats hazel nuts in its underground food store.

Just as the House mouse sometimes goes to live in the countryside, so the Long-tailed Field mouse sometimes enters houses and settles there, though the houses are usually on farms or in villages. The Long-tailed Field mouse does not usually trouble the farmer very much, but it is a great nuisance to the gardener. It digs up his peas and beans and eats his fruit and vegetables. It has been known to invade beehives, kill the bees, eat the honey and wax, and then to make a nest there!

A trio of Field mice in their safe nest underground.

Occasionally the Long-tailed Field mouse population climbs to a peak. The mice can then do much damage on farms. Sometimes they eat off the blades of young corn in spring and almost destroy the crop.

A mouse very similar to the Long-tailed Field mouse is the Yellow-necked mouse. It is larger and brighter coloured and has a yellow patch across its chest. It is found only in southern England and Wales, where it lives in the woods and fields that are also inhabited by the

Harvest mice weave their nest in the air round the stalks of wheat or tall weeds.

Long-tailed Field mouse. But we know little about its habits.

The Harvest mouse is a lovely little animal, reddish gold and only just over two inches long. It has a shorter muzzle than most mice, and this, with its short, rounded ears, makes it look almost spherical. Its underparts are white. It has a *prehensile* tail, with which it can grasp cornstalks and twigs.

The Harvest mouse lives in corn fields, or in rough grass and bushes at the edge of fields and woods. In summer it seems to live almost entirely above the ground. It makes a curious little nest, three or four inches in dia-

Right : Harvest mice often climb into hedgerows. Here one is eating an insect it has caught. *Far right :* Chewing on an ear of wheat.

meter, woven around the upper stalks of wheat plants or the stalks of a tall weed, such as thistle or dock. The nest is completely round, like a ball, and is made of soft grass. There is no entrance hole. The grasses are woven together so skilfully that the mouse can push its way through the sides of the next anywhere, and yet the nest is firm enough to hold a family of young mice.

There are several litters per year, each apparently in a different nest. The gestation period is about three weeks, and the young number from four to nine in a litter. They are born blind and naked, open their eyes at about eleven days and are weaned at fifteen days.

During the summer the Harvest mouse is active by day and night. It seems to organize its life in three-hour cycles – three hours of eating and running about followed by three hours of sleep.

In autumn it used to migrate to corn ricks, and make its home there with other mice. Now that there are few ricks in the countryside it spends the winter in underground burrows. Like the Long-tailed Field mouse, it often lays up stores of food for the winter, chiefly of grain and other seeds.

In Britain the Harvest mouse is found chiefly in the southern counties of England, and has become rather rare. In many parts of Europe it is still very common. There it has occasional peak years, when it becomes a real pest.

55

Opposite : This picture shows the prehensile tail in action. It works rather like a fifth leg.

The American White-footed Deer mouse.

8: Some American Mice

Although it belongs to a different scientific family, the Deer mouse of North America is very like the European Long-tailed Field mouse to look at. It has similar habits, too. It lives in groups in gardens, farmland and woodland, and breeds very quickly. The females are mature enough to start breeding when they are about six weeks old. They

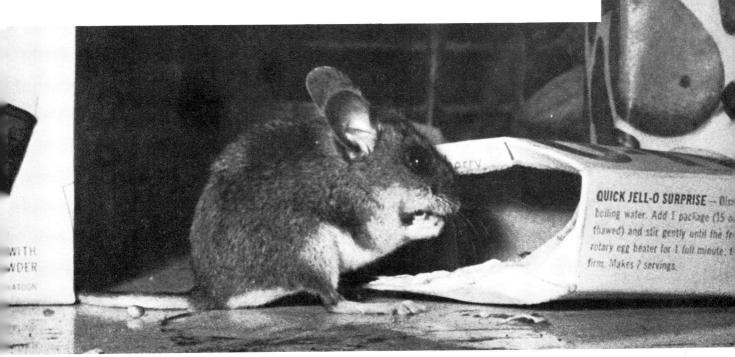

A White-footed Deer mouse up to the usual mouse tricks in the larder!

A Red-backed mouse, another species which lives in America, emerging from its burrow.

produce several litters a year, sometimes with as many as eight or nine young per litter. But Deer mice are not all the same – there are 178 different kinds of them in America!

The American Harvest mouse is like the European Harvest mouse in habits and it makes the same kind of nest, but it is very much larger. It is five inches long, with a tail of about half that length. It is dark brown, also different from its European cousin, with lighter underparts and an orange line along its flanks.

The Grasshopper mouse of western America is unusual

among mice and rats in that it feeds mostly on insects, though it does eat some seeds. There are two species, one brownish red, the other grey. Both are about seven inches long, with short tails.

Except for breeding, the Grasshopper mice make no nests, though they do dig burrows. Most of the time they wander about the countryside, searching for beetles, spiders, and even small lizards and other mice. They seem to hunt by scent and are active mostly at night. Sometimes they will dig out insects hiding underground.

Grasshopper mice are among the few rodents which have any voice other than a squeak. When they are alarmed or annoyed they will bark, like a small dog. And they will also throw back their heads and try to howl. They are very fierce and will try to fight almost any animal they meet.

The Gnome mouse of western America is only two or three inches long. It is a pretty little animal, with an unusually large head and very large, bright eyes. It is dark grey, with cream underparts and a whitish stripe along the side.

The Gnome mouse has cheek pouches in which it stores food that it has to collect quickly. People sometimes see it picking up seeds and stuffing them into its cheek pouches with its tiny paws. It digs burrows, in which it sleeps all day, and comes out to feed by night. It does not really run, but hops instead.

A woodland Jumping mouse. Notice its long, agile hind legs and large paws.

9: Mice in the Tropics

As with rats, mice have adapted themselves to life in most tropical lands, from deep forests to deserts. Mice are among the commonest animals living on the ground in dense rain forests. Most of them are like common European and American mice. Some live on the banks of rivers and lakes and spend their time in and around the water.

The African Climbing mouse makes its nest on the forest floor but spends much of its time climbing in trees and bushes, looking for seeds. It has a prehensile tail to help it.

In the deserts live mice which, like the Kangaroo rats, can live without drinking. One of them is the Australian Hopping mouse, which lives on dry seeds. This little mouse is nocturnal. It has large ears and eyes and long, powerful hind legs. Normally it runs along the ground, searching for food, but when alarmed it makes great leaps, like a kangaroo.

The grassy plains, or *savannahs*, of Africa are inhabited by vast numbers of Zebra mice, or Striped Grass mice. They are tiny animals, with stripes or rows of light spots

Jerboas live in the desert, and race across it with enormous, kangaroo-like leaps.

along their sides. They feed by day in long grass. When disturbed, they leap into the air and then run off at full speed. They look hardly larger than grasshoppers.

The Spotted Grass mouse is about five inches long. It lives in burrows in West Africa and feeds on seeds. The Three-striped mouse, which is about the same size, lives in forests, also in West Africa. It never climbs trees but runs about the forest floor, feeding on fallen fruit. It is greenish brown, with buff underparts and three dark stripes along its back. Like many other mice, it has long hind legs and moves with a series of leaps.

The Pygmy mouse of Africa is only just over two inches long, with a tail of about the same length. It will eat almost anything and live almost anywhere. It is very

common.

A Gerbil. Gerbils are nocturnal, and keep well down in their burrows during the hottest part of the day in the desert and when there are sandstorms.

Jerboas and Gerbils are rodents which are specially adapted for life in desert countries and on grassy plains. Although they belong to different scientific families, jerboas look very like the Kangaroo rats of America. They are small, sandy-coloured animals with very long hind legs, which enable they to speed across the deserts with enormous leaps. They also have long, tufted tails, which help them to balance. They have large bright eyes and come out to feed at night. Although their food consists mainly of dry seeds, they can exist without drinking.

Gerbils are very similar. Most of them live on the savannahs of Africa. The Slender gerbil, which is common enough to cause much damage to crops in West Africa, is five inches long and has a tail three inches longer than itself. It is brownish red, with white underparts; and comes out to feed at night, sleeping by day in small colonies underground.

Another animal like these is the Spring Hare, which is not a hare at all but a rodent like the jerboa. The name is sometimes spelt *Springhaas*, which is not so misleading. It is a much larger animal than the jerboa, about the size of a rabbit, with an astonishing tail nearly two feet long. It spends its day in burrows and comes out to feed by night. When night falls, it comes out with a tremendous leap, in case any enemies are waiting outside.

Jumping mice, with very long tails and hind legs, are also found in America and China.

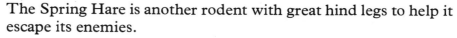

The Spring Hare is another rodent with great hind legs to help it escape its enemies.

10 : The Sleepy Dormouse

The name *Dormouse* means "Sleeping Mouse". It is given to the animal because it sleeps for about six months of each year. In autumn it eats lots of berries, grain and seeds and so puts on a good layer of fat. Then it curls up in a beautifully woven nest of soft grass and goes to sleep for the winter. This habit is called *hibernation*.

The dormouse is more nearly related to the squirrel than to rats and mice, and it looks something like a miniature squirrel. It has a blunt muzzle, large ears, soft fur and a rather bushy tail. Like the squirrel, it often sits on its haunches, holding a nut in its forepaws. It is a golden buff shade, with a white throat and yellowish white underparts. Its length is about three inches, with a tail a little shorter than itself.

For some unknown reason, dormice have become rather rare in England. A hundred years ago, when they were common, children used to catch them and keep them as pets. Most animals do not make good pets if kept in the country where they are caught, but dormice are the exception. They live quite contentedly in captivity, and

they live longer than most mice – sometimes three or four years. As pets, though, they are not very satisfactory because they only wake up and run about at night. And, of course, they spend half the year asleep.

In summer the dormouse makes a nest fairly high above above the ground in bushes, to sleep in during the day. Its winter nest is underground, at the roots of trees or under leaf litter.

Like most mice, the dormouse produces several litters a year. There are usually only three or four young per litter, however. The young are born blind and naked and do not open their eyes until they are eighteen days old. They are not fully independent before they are about six weeks old. The gestation period is three weeks.

Although so sleepy by day, at night the dormouse is very active and agile. It climbs exceptionally well. It feeds on insects and occasionally birds' eggs, as well as on nuts, fruit, berries and sometimes the bark of trees.

Besides fattening up in autumn, so that it is often twice its springtime weight, it lays up a store of food for winter use. Although it sleeps so soundly, it does wake up now and again and has a meal. During hibernation the body temperature of the dormouse drops from the normal 94°F. to only 39°F.

Another kind of dormouse, the Edible or Fat dormouse, was introduced to England eighty or ninety years ago. A few were released by Lord Rothschild in his park

67

Opposite : Although so sleepy, dormice are also quite agile.

near Tring, Hertfordshire, and they have spread to many Midland counties.

The Fat dormouse is larger than the dormouse – about seven inches long, with a bushy tail of the same length. It is silvery grey and lives mostly in trees, but comes into barns, storehouses and even houses in autumn and winter. The name "Edible Dormouse" was given to it because the Romans used to fatten it for eating. The Romans thought it was a great delicacy.

There are plenty of dormice and Fat dormice in Europe. There are so many Fat dormice in some countries of southern Europe that they are pests. Southern Europe also has another dormouse, the Garden or Oak dormouse, which is about four inches long, with a tail the same length. It is a pretty creature, with greyish white fur and white underparts.

The Cape dormouse and the African dormouse, which live in Africa, are very like the dormouse in habits, and the African dormouse looks like it, too. The Cape dormouse is rather larger and has soft, silvery fur with a white tail. The Japanese dormouse is also very like the European kind. In South-east Asia is a dormouse called the Blind dormouse, because it lives inside rotten logs and hardly ever needs to use its eyes, which are therefore very small.

Above : In its most usual position—curled up and fast asleep.
Below : A Garden dormouse creeps cautiously out of a hollow tree.

70   These two pictures show how much larger dormice are than
other mice and voles. The dormouse has come across a little food
store of nuts which the Field mouse has collected.

But the smaller animal is not afraid, and holds its own against the dormouse.

11: The Mysterious Mole-rat

Africa and southern Europe have some curious little animals called Mole-rats. They are not moles, which are insect-eaters, and are more closely related to rats, which are rodents. But they look and behave rather like moles.

Mole-rats are subterranean animals, living entirely underground. They cannot see or hear, because their eyes and ears are completely covered with skin. They find their way and examine their surroundings by their sense of touch.

Mole-rats cannot see or hear, and spend almost the whole of their lives underground.

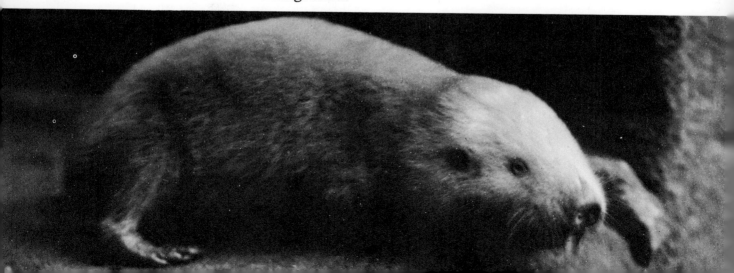

The mole has great, spade-like front paws with which to dig, but the mole-rat does much of its digging with its enormous front teeth. It also has a hard, horny muzzle with which it pushes its way through the earth. Its body is streamlined, and it has very thick fur.

The Mediterranean mole-rat is about eleven inches long and has no tail. It digs a whole maze of burrows, throwing up the soil it has dug out in heaps, as the mole does. In this subterranean home are nesting chambers, store rooms, feeding areas and even latrines. The mole-rat eats roots, tubers and bulbs, some of which it collects and stores.

The African mole-rats, of which there are many kinds, are mostly smaller. The West African mole-rat, like the Mediterranean mole-rat, has no eyes and ears, but most species have tiny eyes. Strong claws on their forefeet help them with digging, but they rely mainly on their teeth, which are very large and powerful.

The West African mole-rat is about six inches long and is covered with short, soft, pinkish-orange fur. The Kenya mole-rat is seven or eight inches long, and its fur is golden-brown. Its teeth are bright orange. Most of the mole-rats like sandy soil best, as it is easy to tunnel in; the Cape mole-rat, which lives in South Africa, is known also as the Sand mole. This mole-rat is regarded as a pest in gardens.

Most curious of all is the Naked mole-rat, which has no

fur at all. Its skin is pinkish grey, like that of a baby rat before its fur starts to grow. It certainly does not need any covering, for it lives underground, in hot semi-desert in northern Kenya and Somalia.

Although most people dislike them and think they do nothing but bad, rats and mice occupy an important place in the world of nature. They feed on the world's plant life, and in turn carnivorous animals and birds feed on them. Without them there would be few owls, hawks, cats, weasels, mink and many other interesting creatures. And, as we have seen, rats and mice are fascinating creatures themselves: naturalists admire them for their intelligence and their ability to adapt to different surroundings, which is why, in spite of having so many enemies, they have survived and spread over six continents. We do not often realize it, but nature would be poorer without them.

Glossary

BLACK DEATH. A disease, also known as the bubonic plague, which swept through Europe in the middle of the fourteenth century. About a third of the population died.

BUBONIC PLAGUE. Another name for the Black Death. It was carried by rat fleas.

BURROWS. Holes in the ground dug by the animals which live in them.

CARNIVORES. Flesh-eating animals, such as cats, lions, wolves and bears.

GESTATION. The period between mating and the birth of a baby animal; the period during which the baby is carried in its mother's body.

GREGARIOUS. Sociable. Animals which live in groups or communities are called gregarious.

HIBERNATION. A period of sleep during winter.

INCISORS. Front teeth, or cutting teeth; in rodents they are very powerful and are protected by a covering of hard enamel.

LITTER. A brood of animals, all born at one time.

MORTALITY RATE. The proportion of an animal population dying within a certain period of time.

MIGRATION. The movement of an animal from one place to another. It is usually seasonal, as when a bird migrates from England to Africa in autumn, or when mice migrate from the open fields to buildings as winter approaches.

NOCTURNAL. Night-loving. A nocturnal animal is one which is active only at night.

PARASITE. A creature which makes its home on another animal's body. Rats have fleas as parasites.

POPULATION EXPLOSION. Certain animals experience population cycles. From a low level the population increases rapidly until it reaches a peak. The climax is a population explosion. Thereafter disasters of various kinds usually force the population back down to normal again. The whole cycle will usually take a number of years, and then repeats itself.

PREHENSILE. Able to seize. A prehensile tail is one which can be used as an extra hand, to grasp a twig or branch.

RODENT. A group of animals which have two pairs of long and sharp front teeth, especially suited for gnawing. Rats and mice are rodents, and so are squirrels.

SAVANNAH. Hot grassy plains in Africa.

SPHERICAL. Shaped like a sphere or ball.

SUBTERRANEAN. Underground.

TERRITORY. An area of land which an animal looks on as its

own property. Animals will often drive other animals of the same species from their territory.

WADI. A dry watercourse, in desert country in Asia and Africa. It carries water only after heavy rain, which does not come often.

Finding Out More

Most rats and mice are nocturnal. Sometimes when they know of a good food supply and have used it undisturbed for a long time they will venture out by day. Otherwise we can see then by day only if we disturb them in their sleeping quarters.

On farms, if a corn rick is being threshed or a wood pile demolished, or sacks or bales moved in a barn, some rats or mice are almost sure to be disturbed. These are likely to be the common Brown rat and the House mouse.

The best way of seeing the less common kinds of mouse is to find where the mice are feeding (as on peas sown in the garden!), feed them with titbits left nearby for a few nights, and then fix up an electric light which can be switched on by remote control to shine on the bait. You should then be able to watch them at their meal.

It is easy to make a simple boxlike trap to catch mice alive. Most mice are easily tamed. They should be given a warm hutch, with a separate sleeping compartment.

Even simpler, if you wish to study mouse behaviour and do not mind which kind of mouse you study, is to buy tame mice from the pet shop.

Most larger zoos have rodent houses, where the rats and mice from foreign countries may be seen.

Books to read:—

The Living World of Animals (Readers Digest Association).

British Mammals, by L. Harrison Matthews (Collins).

Systematic Dictionary of Mammals of the World, by Maurice Burton (Museum Press).

The Oxford Book of Vertebrates, by Marion Nixon (Oxford).

Pets, Usual and Unusual, by Maxwell Knight (Routledge & Kegan Paul).

Mammals of Britain: their Tracks, Trails and Signs, by M. J. Lawrence and R. W. Brown (Blandford).

Animal Life of the British Isles, by Edward Step (Warne).

Small Mammals of West Africa, by A. H. Booth (Longmans).

Control of Rats and Mice, by R. A. Davis (HMSO Bulletin 181, 1970).

Picture Credits

The publishers would like to thank the following for permission to reproduce copyright pictures: Natural History Photographic Agency, *frontispiece*, pp. 10, 12, 22, 23, 24, 30, 34, 63; Mary Evans Picture Library, *title page*, p. 16; Ardea Photographics, pp. 6, 56; Rentokil, pp. 8, 9, 19, 20, 25; Frank Lane, pp. 11, 15, 35, 36, 60, 67, 69, 70, 71; Bruce Coleman Ltd, pp. 26, 27, 29, 57, 58; Paul Popper Ltd, pp. 31, 32, 44, 46, 62, 64, 72; Leslie Jackman, pp. 37, 40, 48, 50, 51, 52, 53, 54; Heather Angel, pp. 42, 43, 49.

Index

Africa, 20, 32, 33, 37, 61–3, 68, 72, 76, 77
African climbing mouse, 61
African dormouse, 68
Alexandrine rat, 30
America, 17, 18, 36, 37, 57–9, 63, 64
American harvest mouse, 58
Antarctica, 18, 39
Arctic, 8
Asia, 20, 68, 77
Atlantic, 18, 40
Australia, 37
Australian hopping mouse, 61

Black Death, 19, 28, 75
Black rat, 17–20, 26–31, 35, 39, 43
Blind dormouse, 68
Britain, 17, 28, 55
Brown rat, 10–12, 17, 19, 21–5, 27–8, 30–1, 33, 35, 39, 43, 46, 78
bubonic plague, 28, 30, 75

Canada, 18
Cane rat, 32, 33
Cape mole-rat, 73
cats, 14, 26, 46, 74, 75
Central America, 35
Central Asia, 17, 18, 39
China, 64
cold stores, 39, 40
Cotton rat, 35, 37
crows, 14

Deer mouse, 56–8
Desert rat, 35
dogs, 14, 26
Dormouse, 7, 65–71

East Africa, 33
Edible dormouse, 67–8
England, 17, 51, 55, 65, 67, 76
Europe, 17, 18, 19, 28, 30, 35, 39, 55, 68, 72, 75

Fat dormouse, 67–8
foxes, 14, 26

Galapagos Islands, 40
Garden dormouse, 68, 69
Gerbil, 63
gestation, 13, 44, 49, 55, 67, 75
Giant pouched rat, 33, 34
Giant rat, 33
Gnome mouse, 59
Grasshopper mouse, 58, 59

Harvest mouse, 52–5, 58
hawks, 14, 26, 74
hibernation, 65, 75
House mouse, 11, 13, 38–47, 50, 78

incisors, 7
India, 30

Japanese dormouse, 68
Jerboa, 62–4
Jumping mouse, 60, 64

Kangaroo rat, 36–7, 61, 63
Kenya, 74
Kenya mole-rat, 73

London, 30, 39
Long-tailed field mouse, 15, 47–52, 55, 57

Mediterranean mole-rat, 73
mole, 72, 73
mole-rat, 72, 73
mongoose, 26
Mosaic-tailed rat, 32

Naked mole-rat, 73
Nile grass rat, 37

Oak dormouse, 68
owls, 14, 15, 26, 74

Pacific, 18
Pack rat, 33, 35
Pygmy mouse, 62

Red-backed mouse, 58
Rice rat, 36
Roof rat, 28
Russia, 17

Sand mole, 73
Sand rat, 37
Scotland, 40
savannah, 61, 63, 76
Ship rat, 28
Slender gerbil, 63
South Africa, 73
South America, 20, 35
Spotted grass mouse, 62
Spring hare, 64
squirrel, 65
Stick-nest rat, 37
stoat, 14, 26, 46
Striped mouse, 61
Swamp rat, 31

Three-striped mouse, 62
Tree rat, 30

United States, 10, 35

wadis, 37, 77
Wales, 51
Water vole, 32
weasels, 26, 46, 74
West Africa, 62, 63
West African mole-rat, 73
West Indies, 8
White rat, 30, 31
Wood mouse, 47, 49

Yellow-necked mouse, 51

Zebra mouse, 61